Blood Along the Niagara

A Guidebook

Battles of the War of 1812
an Hour's Drive from
Niagara Falls

With Maps, Illustrations,
Dates & Locations of
Battle Reenactments

by

Joseph P. Ritz

BookLocker.com, Inc.
2010

Dedicated to my grandson, Joe, whose quiet companionship and comments were helpful in our travels while researching and taking photographs.

TABLE OF CONTENTS

Introduction

For most Americans the imprecisely named War of 1812 has long been America's forgotten war. Even Americans living near Canadian border areas where most of the battles occurred have forgotten it, or reluctantly admit they have never heard of it.

In the 1980s the Buffalo NY Chamber of Commerce put out a brochure commemorating "200 years of peace between Canada and the U.S." apparently unaware that in 1813 British and Canadian troops and their Indian allies burnt down the city.

Even many Canadians express only a vague knowledge of the war, although it was the last fought on Canadian soil. Nevertheless, nearly all the monuments, battlefields and structures dating from the war are to be found on the Canadian side of the Niagara.

It produced the country's most famous military sailing vessel, the U.S. Constitution ("Old Ironsides"), boarded annually by thousands of visitors where it floats in Boston harbor. It inspired the gray uniforms still worn at West Point in honor of an important victory on the Niagara River, where for the first time American troops beat a British force of equal size. In short, the war showed the world that America was an independent nation, growing in power and was not to be trifled with by the major powers. As such, it has been called America's second War of Independence.

It also served to stiffen the resolve of Canadians to become an independent nation, not part of the United States or under the domination of Great Britain.

This book tells about the battles fought within an hour's drive from Niagara Falls. They have many stories to be told, tales of horror, bravery, incompetence, overconfidence and revenge. Most are important for the understanding of the conduct of the war, which was largely fought in the region. This book also aims to give visitors to the Niagara Frontier an idea of the landscape in which the battles were fought.

It points out where surviving structures from the war can be found, including three historic forts. As well, it is a guide to the locations of battlefields, graveyards and not to be missed monuments, including the world's second tallest column honoring a war hero and what many be the most unusual and historic hazard on a golf course.

Because many parents will have children accompanying them as they search out the battle sites within a short drive of the falls, I have enlisted the help of my 12-year-old grandson, who shares my name and my birthday. His view of the places and recreations of battles and as well as military demonstrations are included.

The book is divided by location of sites to enable visitors to visit them with the least amount of driving. As a result, the section of the book dealing with battles and events is divided into those north of the falls, those south of the falls and those in New York State. Fortunately, the division largely parallels the historic course of the war in the Niagara Region. The one exception, is the bloody battle of Lundy's Lane, located within the present limits of the Canadian City of Niagara Falls.

We are also aware that measurements of distance are different in the U.S. and Canada. For this reason, distances are given in both miles and kilometers.

The intention of the writer is that the reader will find this small book not only instructive, and useful but a good and fun read.

To better understand the nature of the battles and the hardships and bravery of those involved, it's useful to understand the tactics and weapons in use at the time.

First, the British "redcoats" and even the Canadian milita were better trained and disciplined than the Americans at the beginning of the war.

Neither side had a large military force in North America. Because of money pinching on the part of many in Congress, the U.S. regular army at the start of the war had only 11,744 officers and men, including 5,000 recruits enlisted in January. when it became apparent that there would be another war between Britain and the U.S. The combined British and Canadian forces were even smaller in numbers — about 7,000.

It should be remembered that both the U.S. and Canada were sparcely settled. The U.S. population was about 7,700,000. The total population of Canada was a liitle below half a million. The woods which mostly covered the countryside in 1812 have been cut down, swamps have been drained, nearly all the houses which you see now were built long after the war, the vast commerical activity, the restaurants, hotels and amusements on the river's banks were not there. The Niagara, however, has changed little in the last 200 years.

In 1812 both armies mainly used the weapons and tactics from the War of Independence. Battles were fought at extremely close range — about 30 feet apart. The inaccurate musket was still the principal weapon. While rifles were sometimes used, they were slower to reload than the musket. The idea was to rip the enemy apart by blasting them with muskets from hundreds of guns. The soldiers would then rush forward at those of the enemy still standing and impale them with bayonets. The men had to be taught to quell their fears of death and pain and line up in ranks shoulder to shoulder. One row of soldiers crouched and reloaded while another line fired over them. If the soldier in front was hit by a musket ball, another one stepped forward to take his place. British soldiers practiced the drill endlessly until it became an automatic reflex. At the war's beginning, that idea was largely foreign for the Americans who had recently enlisted.

What is remarkable about those who fought is not that many soldiers deserted the army or fled the battlefield, but that so many perservered.

Chapter One

The Road to War

When word that war had been declared between the United States and Britain in early summer of 1812, officers from Fort Niagara on the American side of the Niagara were cordially dining with their British counterparts in Fort George just outside of what is now Niagara-on-the-Lake. It was agreed that the meal would continue as though no war existed. Afterwards, the British officers bid the Americans goodbye and good luck as they escorted them to the boats that would take them back to Fort Niagara.

It was late June. Few of the officers on either side thought the war would last past Christmas. There was even hope that peace might yet be possible. Yet, in a few weeks these amiable companions on both sides would be shelling and shooting one another.

It was a war entered into blindly by both sides, neither of which thought it would actually occur, although war hawks on the American side had been urging conflict for nearly a decade. And not without reason.

Britain in the early 1800s had once again begun to treat the United States as a disagreeable and inconsiderate child. Its rights were too often ignored, its belongings treated as though they were of little consequence, its citizens game for capture to be to used to work under harsh discipline on British warships.

And then there were hungry thoughts of Canada, a British colony whose citizens, many Americans believed,. would welcome the opportunity to become part of the U.S. After all, in what is now the Niagara region, three of five settlers were newly arrived Americans, lured there by cheap land. They had no loyalty to Britain and students of the war have suggested it is possible that without the war much of Upper Canada (presently Ontario) would have become another state in the union.

One bloody occurrence which best illustrates the high handedness of Britain toward the United States in that period was the attack on the American frigate, the *Chesapeake* in 1807 bound out of Hampton Roads for the Mediterranean. There are three Americans aboard the *Chesapeake* who have escaped from a British warship after being illegally captured and put to hard work on a British frigate. England, nearing climatic battles against Napoleon, is short of men to man its ships. A fifty-gun British warship, the *Leopard,* its officers aware of the escaped Americans and British deserters aboard the *Chesapeake*, demands that the escapees be returned. The captain of the *Chesapeake* pleads ignorance of the men being aboard. The *Leopard* opens fire with her guns. Twenty-two cannon balls tear into the *Chesapeake* killing three men and wounding 18 others. Among them is the captain, James Barron.

The American ship, badly damaged, strikes her colors and the British board the vessel taking back the three Americans and one British deserter, who is hanged.

The incident infuriates , the American public and brings the U.S. and Britain to the brink of war.

Thomas Jefferson, who is now president, threatens war, but is reluctant. "If the English do not give us the satisfaction we demand, we will take Canada, which wants to join the union."

The president bans British warships from entering American waters and tries to embargo trade with England. But the embargo fails.

"America is no longer a bugbear; there is no terror in her threats," declares Lord Sidmouth, the Lord Privy Seal.

American anger cools, but resentment smolders outside of New England. Yankee merchants and ship owners are engaged in profitable trade with Britain and don't want to see it end. over the hanging of a handful of sailors.

But further west, particularly in new states as Ohio, Kentucky and Indiana, anger swells augmented by fear of American Indians[1]who have ambitions for their own independent nation made up of a large part of Ohio, Indiana and Michigan.

It is believed, with some reason, that the Indians are being encouraged by the British, who are also supplying them with guns.

The Speaker of the House of Representatives, Henry Clay, is the leader of the war hawks. Among the outspoken advocates of war is one of his followers, a Buffalo congressman, Peter B. Porter, chairman of the influential Foreign Relations Committee. Porter will take a leading role in the war on the Niagara Frontier and will eventually profit from it by supplying goods to the army as quartermaster for the New York militia.

By spring of 1812 talk of war with Britain has grown serious. The main issues are the continuing impressment of American sailors to work on British ships and the English ban of American vessels sailing for ports controlled by Napoleon without first paying Britain.

By 1812, some 400 U.S. vessels have been captured on the pretext they are carrying goods to the English enemy. The war hawks in Congress are convinced that, faced with a real

---

The term "Indians" is used in this book, rather than the confusing, but political correct "native Americans" because the Senecas, Shawnees, Iroquois and all the other tribes were called Indians during the War of 1812.

prospect of war and already engaged with a fight with France, Britain will back down when its leaders realize they are serious.

They are young, between the ages of 29 and 36, and lawyers all.

And their blood is hot. They believe that America must avenge the English insults taken for nearly a decade. The means to do that -- if Britain remains stubborn -- is by taking Canada.

President James Madison has dragged his feet when he has been asked to lead the nation to war. He is a man of peace.

He sees the dangers of dividing the nation if a war with Britain should occur. But he has been gradually convinced that there may be no other course. He is willing to declare war if Congress forces his hand.

Britain does not want war any more than the elected American leaders, but it has misjudged American anger, refusing to yield on either of the two issues until it is too late. It responds to the American war hawks' threats by sending three battalions of troops to Canada, but some members in Parliament begin reconsidering the government's stubborn resistance to American demands. Unfortunately, for those who want to settle with America, before action can be taken, the English prime minister, Spencer Perceval, is assassinated on the floor of the House of Commons.

Parliament does eventually repeal the embargo of American trade with France and makes the announcement on June 16. But it is too late. There is no radio or telegraph or satellite communications. On June 18, America declares war without knowing Parliament's action to at least partly satisfy U.S. demands. Besides, the matter of impressment of American sailors remains.

In America, declaration of war is greeted with cheers and boos, riots and the tolling of church bells. John C. Calhoun, one of the most outspoken of the war hawks, and Clay lead their followers in a war dance. " In four weeks most of Canada will be a U.S. possession, Calhoun predicts.

Jefferson is equally optimistic. "We shall strip Great Britain of all her possessions on this continent," he writes.

Looking only at the numbers of troops available on each side, it seems that conquest of Canada is inevitable. Congress has authorized a force of 35 thousand troops. In all of Canada there are only 4,500 British troops. But they are trained and disciplined troops.

It is one thing to authorize a force of 35 thousand, but another to get that many volunteers for a war unpopular in a large segment of the country. But most of all, the U.S. troops will be largely untrained and, at least in the beginning of the war, led largely by political appointees with little or no military experience.

***

Blame John Jacob Astor, at least in part, for the disasters that befall U.S. forces as war begins. The merchant has vast stores of furs in Canada. To protect them, he sends messages to his agents that war has been declared. Astor's messages arrive ahead of those dispatched by the government in Washington to its troops in remote places. It was the 1812 equivalent of email versus snail mail. As a result, the British in those areas are alerted that war has been declared, while the Americans slumber in the happy belief they are at peace.

A small number of British troops and Indians surprise the U.S. garrison on Mackinac Island and capture it without a fight, giving the British control of the routes to the fur country and gaining the alliance of the Indian warriors in the Old Northwest.

Surprise is also a major factor when a Canadian long boat, manned by six seamen armed with pistols, captures a U.S. schooner on Lake Erie. The schooner carries supplies intended for General Hull, who is leading a small army marching to

Detroit. The schooner also carries papers telling of Hull's strength and his plans, should war break out.

But in the end, it makes little difference. Hull overestimates the strength of the weak and small British force before him. When British General Isaac Brock sends him a letter that should there be a battle he will be unable to control his Indian allies, who may well massacre and rape women and children, Hull surrenders Detroit and his troops to Gen. Brock without a fight.

So far, the British have won without a major battle. The first real battle of the war will be held on the Niagara Frontier at Queenston north of Niagara Falls.

Chapter Two

The Battle of Queenston Heights

Five kilometers (about 8 miles) downstream from Niagara Falls, on the Canadian side of the river, a statue of British General Sir Isaac Brock looks down the treacherous and swiftly moving stream from atop a 184-foot column, the second tallest such structure in the world. Only the statue of Admiral Nelson in London's Talfalagar Square is taller. Surrounded by floral gardens, the column marks the location of the final phase of the Battle of Queenston Heights.

It is mid-October; the red, yellow, orange and brown leaves are falling from the forested trees on both sides of the border.

The war is four months old. The British and Canadian forces have the only victories. They are virtually bloodless victories. The Americans have yet to fight.

At the Lewiston, N.Y. side of the river are massed some 7,000 troops awaiting the word to invade Canada. Of them, 1,700 are regular army soldiers. The rest are militia. On the Canadian side, are some 1,700 British soldiers and 600 Canadian militia.

They are thinly scattered along the 36 miles (50 kilometers) of the river except for a few hundred at Fort George outside of the rustic village of Newark, now the upscale cultural and garden community of Niagara-on-the-Lake. Augmenting the British troops are five hundred Mohawk Indians, not a large force, but they strike terror into the hearts and minds of the Americans.

The American forces have been camped near Lewiston since August. Most are untrained militia fresh off the farm who clamor to be allowed to cross the river and defeat the British. It is rainy, windy and chilly. There are not enough tents or even blankets. Sanitation is poor. Many of the American soldiers are too sick to fight. Many are armed only with the muskets they have brought from home. Others have no shoes. Most have not been paid the $8 monthly pay for a private that Congress has allotted — up from $5 monthly before the war.

To encourage enlistment, Congress is also offering a recruitment bounty of $31 plus three months pay and 160 acres of land.

The American troops waiting on the eastern bank of the Niagara, however, have not only not been paid but some have been fed very little. They demand to fight or they will go home. The number of deserters increases daily. The impetuous challenge of the raw soldiers is in part provoked by Peter Porter, now quartermaster of the New York militia, who spreads rumors that their leader, Stephen Van Rensselaer, is a coward, afraid to engage the enemy.

Indeed, Van Rensselaer, the last Dutch patroon in New York, a man who controls a vast estate outside of Albany, opposes the war. He is a leading Federalist politician, who wants to become governor. Despite having no military experience, he has been appointed by Governor Daniel Tompkins to head the invading force. It is a political masterstroke. Van Rensselaer cannot refuse the post without hurting his political ambitions. If he is successful, he will not be able to resign his command honorably. If he loses, he will be disgraced.

The attack is planned for Oct. 11, but has to be delayed two days when an American officer deserts and makes off with all the oars for the boats.

The initial objective is Queenston heights, a steep bluff rising some 300 feet just south of the village of Queenston, only five miles downstream from the falls. They will have to cross the dangerous, swiftly moving river in row boats.

The American force is too big not to have been noticed by the British.

Brock has strengthened the force in Queenston and put a large cannon high on Queenston Heights commanding a view of the river.

The river is 1,250 feet wide at the point of crossing and once the troops succeed in crossing the swirling water, they will have to ascend rocky and heavily wooded slopes on the Queenston side -- all under cannon and musket fire.

At 3 a.m. on Oct.13th, the Americans take to the boats and begin crossing the river in a heavy rain. There are some 600 men in the first wave.. They are in two large boats, each holding 80 men, and a dozen large rowboats, each holding t wenty-five.

The British sight them before they land. The Americans are met with a hail of musket fire and shrapnel from cannon fire both in Queenston and from the heights.

Ten of the boats make the beach, the others are swept downstream. The 300 or so American troops who have landed at Queenston are being killed and wounded from musket and cannon fire. Especially deadly are the balls and grape from the cannon on the heights.

The Americans are pinned on the beach. But, a 23-year-old captain, John E. Wool, has heard of a narrow fishermen's path which leads up the heights. Despite being wounded, he finds the path and leads his men up it. As dawn breaks, they find Brock himself directing the cannon fire with only handful of soldiers, the rest having been sent to down to help repulse the invaders in Queenston. The British troops, led by Brock, hurriedly spike the cannon and flee down the heights.

Brock retreats to Queenston where he rallies 200 men to follow him up the heights. He leads a charge. But the Americans have been reinforced. There are now several hundred American troops on the heights. The British charge fails. Brock leads a second charge. An American soldier sends a musket ball through his heart. The British retreat carrying Brock's body with them.

Brock's aide, Col. John Macdonell, acting attorney-general of the providence, leads yet another attempt to retake the heights. But like his general, McDonnell is killed leading the charge and the British again retreat.

Lt. Col. Winfield Scott, a six foot, five-inch giant, a regular army officer who will emerge as one of the heroes of the war, takes over command of the heights from the wounded Wool.

The Americans appear to have won the battle. They occupy the village and the heights. All that is required is that the reserve force of a couple of a thousand New York militia cross the river and join the battle.

But the militia, who had been clamoring for a fight a few hours before, now remember that their enlistment requires them only to protect New York State.

America's Founding Fathers had not contemplated invading another country. The state militia, under a strict interpretation of the law, can only be used
in defense of the nation.

The militia will not cross the river to fight in a foreign country despite the pleas from their officers. They have seen the dead and wounded being returned by boat, men with missing legs and arms, some blinded, some with their guts hanging out of their stomachs. They have heard their screams of pain and the war hoops of scalping Indians.

The British still have cannon capable of hitting anyone crossing the river. They include a massive 24-pounder at what is now Vrooman's Point, a few miles north of Queenston.

The New York militia have lost their taste for battle.

On the heights, the Americans are doomed. Without needed reinforcements from the New York side of the river and running short of ammunition they have no choice but surrender. They are all taken prisoner, including the 26-year-old Scott.

So ends the Battle of Queenston, an inglorious ending for the Americans, a triumph to be celebrated by the British and Canadians.

Today, visitors can climb the 235 steps inside the Brock monument for a spectacular view of the area where the two sides fought and of Niagara Falls to the north. The monument and park are just north of the famous floral clock. They are hard to miss if you drive along the splendid, scenic Niagara Parkway, that follows the path of the military road used in 1812.

The park, beribboned with planted flowers in warm weather, is now a place for families to picnic. You can buy food at a nearby snack bar. Or you can dine in the upscale and much praised Queenston Heights Restaurant in the shadow of the monument. It serves excellent food and wine and a gorgeous view high above the river.

A wading pool for tots is set in the middle of grass-covered mounds, all that remains of Fort Drummond, occupied later in the war by soldiers from both sides as they continued to fight over the heights.

Among the plaques in a wall near the restaurant is one honoring the "Colored Corps," a force of free blacks and escaped slaves who, fearing being returned to their masters in the United States, fought with the British during the Battle of Queenston. Among the other plaques is one honoring Sir Roger

Hale Sheaffe who took over command of the British-Canadian forces after the death of Brock and led a flank march which eventually drove the Americans from the heights.

Continuing a few hundred yards along the Niagara Parkway is a scenic parking area overlooking the river. To the left of the parking area is a path and a wooden staircase that leads to the site of the redan which held cannon captured by the Americans.

A replica of the cannon is located on the site. At the bottom of the steep incline off Queenston Road to the right is a stone monument with a British Union Jack flying over it. It marks the place where General Brock died. In a glass case nearby is a scaled-down statue of Brock's horse, Alfred.

In Queenston are a few houses that were present when the battle was fought. One of them is the Laura Secord House, named after a Canadian heroine of the war.

Born in Massachusetts, Laura Ingersoll came to the Niagara Peninsula with her parents after the American Revolution and married James Secord, a member of the Canadian militia who was seriously wounded during the battle. When the fighting ended, Laura brought her husband back to their home and nursed him to health.

Laura became a legend a year later when, when she learned the Americans were planning to ambush a small British force 20 miles (32 kilometers) away. The 38-year-old mother of five, walked and ran through dense woods and a dangerous swamp to warn the British. The young man in charge, Lt. James Fitzgibbon, laid a trap for the Americans and after a fierce engagement was successful in bluffing the much larger American force into surrendering on the belief they were outnumbered. There are several stories of how Laura learned of the planned American attack. She herself told many versions, among them that the Americans were dining at her house. (At the time the U.S. forces were temporarily in command of the area, after having taken Fort George. That battle is described in the following chapter.) What is certain is that Laura emerged as a hero north of the border. Americans might look on her differently.

While you are in Canada, try Laura Secord candies. They are delicious!

The restored Secord home, at Partition and Queen streets in Queenston, is open during tourist season from April to October. Guides in period costume describe the house and tell of her adventure. Admission is charged.

To see the river shore where the American troops landed, take the road leading to the boat ramp at the end of Dunfries Street. The steep riverbanks are covered with brush and trees much as they were in 1812. A dirt and gravel road near the northern end of Queenston Street also leads to the river.

Three miles further north on the Niagara Parkway is a plaque marking the location of Vrooman's Battery. There is, alas, little on the U.S. side of the river to mark where VanRensselaer's army encamped before embarking for Queenston.

But then, Americans lost the battle.

Chapter Three

Fort George Changes Hands -
The Burning of Niagara-on-the-Lake

As 1812 comes to an end, Americans are realizing victory in the war is not a matter of simply marching into Canada. The only American soldiers in Canada are prisoners of war.

As a new year begins, the United States is still looking for a victory on the battlefield. It is largely a warm weather war. Neither side wants to fight in the northern cold. Besides, troops can't cross the border in boats until ice is off the lakes and rivers.

The campaign of 1813 doesn't get underway until the end of April. On April 26, some 1,400 American troops, carried in 14 ships that have sailed nearly the length of Lake Ontario, land at York, now the modern metropolis of Toronto.

Their object is to capture two large war ships being built by the British in Toronto's harbor, the largest of which is named the Isaac Brock..

 With the ships added to the American fleet, it is hoped U.S. control of Lake Ontario will be assured. Control of the lake will cut off supplies to troops on the Niagara Peninsula.

The American invaders are under the command of Brigadier General Zebulon Montgomery Pike, after whom Pike's Peak is named, although the 34-year-old Pike is not the first white man to discover it, nor has he climbed it.

Pike is sympathetic to the Canadians, who he believes are victims of the British as much as the Americans. Plundering of homes, he tells his men, will result in death for the offenders.

"The unoffending citizens of Canada are many of them our own countrymen, and the poor Canadians have been forced into this war."

The city is captured and its Parliament and other public buildings burned -- the British will later burn Washington D.C. in retaliation. But Pike's moment of glory is just that. He is killed by a boulder when fleeing British troops blow up a powder magazine. With Pike dead, the command forbidding plundering of private homes is ignored by many of the soldiers. As for the British ships sought by the Americans, the Isaac Brock is burned by the British, the other ship sails away.

But the stage is set for the capture of Fort George. The attack comes on May 27, after cannons from Fort Niagara, across the Niagara River and 16 American warships carrying 4,500 men have shattered much of the fort. The naval cannon fire is directed by a young officer, Oliver Hazard Perry, who is to gain fame by defeating a British fleet in the Battle of Lake Erie which occurs further west.

The landing force attacking Fort George is led by Col. Winfield Scott, freed by the British in a prisoner exchange, and now seeking revenge for the defeat at Queenston. He is in charge of 20 small boats containing 800 men and a six pound cannon.

The Americans scale a 12 foot bank under British fire and together with a second wave of 1,500 troops, drive back the British and Canadian troops, outnumbered by invading Americans by four to one. Fort George is evacuated and blown up by the British troops, who flee southward following the path of today's Niagara Parkway.

The British have lost 350 men killed, wounded or captured. American losses amount to 150.

Scott, despite a collar bone broken from flying debris when Fort George is blownup, leads the Americans in pursuit of the British-Canadian army. But he is halted by his cautious superiors and the British regulars and Canadian militia flee westward to the high ground of Burlington Heights outside of the present city of Hamilton. The Americans take abandoned Fort Erie without a fight and , for the present, have control of virtually all the Niagara Peninsula.

By June the Americans have advanced to Forty Mile Creek some 30 miles west of the present village of Niagara-on-the-Lake. The Americans have control of the
Niagara Peninsula, but the British army has escaped and this will make the capture of Fort George meaningless.

On June 4 some 2,600 American troops are marching west from Fort George with the aim of eliminating the 700-man British force at Burlington Heights near the present city of Hamilton. Nearing the enemy, the Americans camp outside the village of Stoney Creek. They are led by two generals, who like too many American officers at the beginning of the war, owe their appointments to politics. Neither of the pair, John Chandler, a former tavern keeper and congressman, and William Winder, a former Baltimore lawyer, have much military experience.

Nevertheless, the only hope of avoiding defeat by an overwhelming force,it seems to the outnumbered British, is a surprise attack. A young, bold British officer, Lt. James Fitzgibbon, disguises himself as a peddler and enters the American camp noting the positions of guns and the layout of the camp. He tells them to his commander Lt. Col. John Harvey, who is planning a night attack on the Americans. (This is the same Fitzgibbon who Laura Secord will alert to American plans after her 20-mile trek.)

A 19-year-old Canadian, Billy Green, whose parents come from New Jersey, has been given the password to go though the American lines by his brother-in-law, who has received it from American officers on the mistaken belief he is loyal to the U.S. Billy runs to Burlington Heights and gives the password to the British. Since he knows the countryside well, young Billy Green leads them on the attack on the early morning of June 5.

It catches the Americans by surprise and routs them. There is a great deal of confused firing in which friend and foe often have a hard time determining which is which. Both Chandler and Winder stumble on to British-Canadian troops in the dark and are captured.

When dawn breaks, both sides leave the field, thinking the other side has won. The British have lost more men, 200, compared to 150 for the Americans, but they retire in order. The Americans panic. They flee the area leaving their dead, cannons, tents and stores. Poorly led, they have suffered another inglorious defeat at the hands of a much smaller force.

The American retreat continues. On June 9, the demoralized Americans burn Fort Erie and abandon it. They join their brother soldiers behind the walls of Fort George for the remainder of the summer. It will be their prison until winter forces them back to American soil. The Niagara peninsula this summer and fall is now largely a no-man's land.

Fitzgibbon organizes a guerrilla force of some 50 men who harass the American troops when they leave the shelter of the fort. An even larger guerrilla force, made up largely of Canadians supporting the Americans, is organized by a former Fort Erie surgeon who has moved to Buffalo, Dr. Cyrenous Chapin. His men and other guerrilla forces plunder the homes of Canadians loyal to the British.

Often the raids are for past personal affronts, rather than for military reasons.

The second year of the war gives Americans some reason to cheer. Thanks to Perry's defeat of the British fleet, Lake Erie is no longer a British lake by which it can supply and reinforce its troops along the Detroit River.

With the aid of Perry's ships, Gen. William Henry Harrison, the future president, has caught and defeated the British-Canadian force retreating from Detroit.

He and his men travel as far east as Fort George, where they camp for several weeks.

But as 1813 nears its end, Harrison and his troops have gone. The American commander in charge of Fort George, George McClure, hears that the British are on their way to recapture it.

McClure is a former judge who is more a New York politician than military leader. He panics. He decides the fort can no longer be defended. All the New York militia under his command have returned to the warmth of their homes on the other side of the river despite his pleas and threats and offer of extra pay. To defend the fort, McClure has only 70 regular soldiers plus about 100 Canadian volunteers sympathetic to the American side.

There is no large British force advancing on the fort. However, McClure believes rumors that say there is. He decides to abandon the fort, but first he gives the ill-conceived order to burn the homes, churches and public buildings in Newark, ignoring the angry protests of Dr. Chapin.

It is a cold and snowy December 10 when McClure gives the order. It is a cruel and senseless task without any military need.

Only women and children and frail old men remain in the village. Some are too ill to leave their homes. Among them is

Mrs. William Dickson, who lives in the first brick house in the village that contains one of the finest libraries in Upper Canada. She is carried out of her house bed and all and dropped into the snow while the soldiers burn the house, clothing, paintings and furniture. The library is not spared. A thousand books, purchased in England, go up in flames.

Ninety-eight houses are destroyed and their 400 occupants left without shelter. Two babies will be born this night in the smoking village.

Besides the homes, barns and stables, two churches are torched before the Americans flee to the New York side of the Niagara. All public buildings, including the court house and library, are smoldering ruins.

Is is said by some historians that it is the cruel and unnecessary burning of Newark, rather than the earlier burning of the public buildings of York, that gives the British reason to burn Washington.

When the first British and Canadian troops arrive on the scene that night they are filled with a strong desire for revenge that they will soon satisfy on the New York side of the river.

That story will be in the next part of this book.

Fort George was battered during the war and neglected afterward, but in 1937 the Providence of Ontario restored the fort to its 1812 appearance. During the summer cannon and musket firing demonstrations, as well as military marches and music of the time, are performed by men and women in period military costume. The fort is open everyday from May 1 through Oct. 31 and weekends in April and November. As of this writing admission for adults was $11.70, $10.05 for seniors, and $5.80 for a child over 5. Young children under 5 are free. The family rate is $29.90 All amounts are in Canadian dollars.

A mound of stones placed by the Historic Sites and Monuments Board of Canada marks where the American troops led by Scott landed before taking Fort George. It is located at the extreme western end of the Niagara-on-the-Lake Golf Course.

Also on the course is the main building of another fort left from the War of 1812, Fort Mississauga, constructed in 1814 after the British had retaken Fort George. It had a better view and command of the lake. No battles were fought there, but it's an interesting structure. At one time, golfers had to shoot over it to reach the green on the other side -- talk about water holes and sand traps!

The course has since been changed to allow today's golfers to avoid the Mississauga hazard.

The Village of Niagara-on-the-Lake (the name dates from the 1890s) today is much prettier and sophisticated than the old rural village of Newark. It is known for its lavish gardens and lovely houses and mansions along its main streets and for excellent restaurants and fine regional wines and jellies. It attracts some 3 million visitors annually.

One of North America's best repertory theater companies, the Shaw Festival, is largely responsible for the number of tourists as well as for the upscale hotels and restaurants in the village. Besides plays by George Bernard Shaw, it presents murder mysteries, musicals by composers like Cole Porter and George Gershwin and dramatic works by such renowned playwrights as Eugene O'Neill, George Abbott, Oscar Wilde and J.M. Synge in its three theaters.

The largest of the theaters, the Festival Theater, is across from Fort George. The theater season runs from April to December.

One of the establishments which has benefited from the Shaw Festival is the Angel Inn, at 224 Regent St., near the

Court House. (www.angel-inn.com). It's the oldest of the hotels and the most historically accurate. It claims its own ghost from the War of 1812. According to the tales told, the ghost is a young British captain killed in the basement of the Inn, who reappears to guests from time to time.

The inn was burned along with the rest of the village, but the present structure was built over the old basement. Young couples wishing to start or add to a family, might be tempted to try sleeping in the Fertility Bed in one of the guest rooms.

The inn also has a pub and restaurant.

The much larger and lavishly appointed Prince of Wales Hotel on Queen Street serves an English high tea late in the afternoon which is well worth the experience.

The only structure of note in the area which survived the War of 1812 is the McFarland House located a 10-minute drive From Niagara-on-the-Lake on the Niagara Parkway. It was used first as a headquarters for the British, then as a hospital for wounded soldiers on both sides.

When it is open from mid-May to early September, it may be toured. Light lunches, teas and wine are served on outside tables. The red brick Georgian structure sits on a small hill flanked by trees, picnic areas and a playground.

For those wishing to stop and picnic, there is outside running water and washroom facilities.

Incidentally, picnic lunches can be bought at several establishments in Niagara-on-the-Lake, including the McFarland House.

Many beautiful homes along the Parkway and in Niagara-on-the-Lake have become bed and breakfast establishments in which friendly hosts and hostess serve gourmet breakfasts. The village's Chamber of Commerce operates a reservation system for the community's hotels and b&b's on its web site: www.niagaraonthelake.com.

Reservations can also be made at the Chamber's offices in the old Court House on Queen Street: Box 1043, Niagara-on-the Lake LOS 1J0.

The Niagara-on-the-Lake Bed and Breakfast Association's web site is: www.bba.notl.pn.ca.

An organization calling itself B&B Concierge Niagara-on-the-Lake, will make reservations for b&b's, theater tickets, dining, golf and wine tours. Website:www.bbstay.ca.

Here are a couple more web sites where housing information can be obtained and reservations made:

www.accomodationsniagara.com
www.hallmarkproperties.net.

For a listing of plays, restaurants and places to stay click the web site of the Shaw Festival (www.shawfest.com).

Some 50 kilometers west (30 miles) the Stony Creek battlefield has been largely absorbed by the growing metropolis of Hamilton. What is left includes the Gage house, now known as the "Battlefield House."

Nearby, the sorry American generals Winder and Chandler pitched their tents before being roused from their sleep by the attacking British.

The house is open to the public. During the summer, guides dressed in colonial costumes take visitors on a tour of the house, which still bears the marks of cannon balls. They also explain the battle to the delight of Canadians.Americans are generally less enthused.

There is also a museum and a gift shop.

Battlefield House is located in the Town of Stony Creek at the intersection of King Street and Route 20, not far from the

QEW super highway. A 100-foot monument marking the battlefield is in front of the house.

Another monument, this one in a cemetery at King Street and Centennial Parkway, honors Billy Green, who gave the American password to the British; and Col. Harvey, who conceived and led the attack.

Col. Harvey was so highly regarded in the Hamilton area that a park on Burlington Heights is named for him.

Some of the British fortifications remain in the area and various sites are marked by plaques and by a cannon from the period.

Most of the remains of fortifications are in Hamilton Cemetery, across from the park.

Burlington Heights is reached from York Street, in the City of Hamilton.

A small military museum next to Dundurn Castle on York Street in the heart of downtown Hamilton contains displays that describe the Battle of Stoney Creek.

Dundurn Castle did not exist in the War of 1812 period. It was built in 1834 by Allan McNab, who at 16 took part in the capture of Fort Niagara and later became prime minister.

The "Castle" is worth a visit itself. Guided tours are offered by costumed guides. There is a restaurant inside and a large garden outside.

A 20-minute drive away is the massive and beautiful Royal Botanical Gardens. (It is so large that buses are required to take visitors to all the gardens.)

To see them adequately would require an extra day, and worth it. But even a quick tour when the flowers are in bloom is rewarding.

The Town of Grimsby, off the Queen Elizabeth Highway in Ontario has a stone monument by Forty Mile Creek marking where the American force, retreating after its defeat at Stoney

Creek, tried to make a stand, but after being attacked, retreated back to Fort George.

Chapter Four

Flames Across the Niagara

It takes little more than a week for the British and Canadians to enact revenge for the needless burning of Newark. British Lt. Gen. Gordon Drummond has come from York (now Toronto) to mastermind the attack across the river.

On the moonless night of December 18, a force of 560 British and Canadian troops embark from a ravine near the McFarland house and silently cross the Niagara in boats rowed by men using muffled oars. They land at Youngstown across the river at a location known as Five Mile Meadows.

An American sentry outside a Youngstown tavern is overpowered and the password demanded. He gives it and is immediately bayoneted. The same fate befalls the 20 American pickets who have taken shelter inside the tavern.

The Brits and Canadians continue their silent march over the snow to the main gate of Fort Niagara. They find the drawbridge down for the changing of the guard. The password is given to the sole sentry, who is then strangled.

The British and Canadians race across the drawbridge to find most of the 460 American troops asleep. There is a brief fight in which 65 Americans are killed and 16 wounded, all by bayonet. The British and Canadians suffer six dead, five wounded. Nearly 400 Americans are captured, along with their 15 officers. The fort, with its 29 cannon, seven thousand muskets and rifles and a vast amount of supplies and clothing, is now in British hands.

At 5 a.m. a cannon shot from the fort tells Major General Phineas Riall on the Canadian side of the river that the bastion has been taken. It is also a signal for Riall to cross the river with a thousand men and 500 Indians and descend on the village of Lewiston, across the river from Queenston. The town is burned and a few citizens scalped by Indians. Within a day, every home and barn from Fort Niagara to the Tonawanda Creek, just north of the present City of Buffalo are put to the torch and their inhabitants left homeless. They include the City of Manchester, now Niagara Falls, N.Y. This is revenge with little pity for the innocent.

The citizens of Buffalo rightfully blame McClure, who has taken his militia to their community. As he marches down Main Street at the head of his troops, shots are fired at him by Chapin's men. Chapin is jailed, but he is freed by a group of angry citizens.

After burning Lewiston and Manchester, the British return to the Canadian side of the Niagara.

The citizens of Buffalo breathe a sigh of relief, thinking their community has been saved. Many thanks are given to God at Christmas services.

However, on Dec. 30, the British-Canadian forces and their Indian allies again cross the river. The militia, on whom the citizens were depending for protection, flee without offering much of a defense. Untrained, and without military discipline, they realized they might be killed and scalped. Most became as reluctant to fight in New York state as they were to fight in Canada.

The British forces take and burn Black Rock and then proceed south to Buffalo. Chapin appears before the advancing troops carrying a white flag and offering to surrender the city, provided it be spared.

Since he has no official standing in the community, the British take him prisoner and proceed to burn the village.

Sarah Lovejoy, a 35-year-old mother whose husband is in the militia, decides to stay in her Main Street home and protect her belongings. When Indians break into her house and start rummaging through her possessions, she struggles with them.

They kill and scalp her.

In most cases, Buffalonians flee their homes before they are looted and burned. One woman, Mrs. Margaret St. John, a widow, saves her small story-and-one-half cottage at Main and Mohawk Streets, by imploring the British not to burn it. But they burn the barn and the main St. John house across the street, which she has been operating as a hotel since her husband drowned the previous year.

Two other buildings are also spared because they are made of stone and will not burn: the jail and the blacksmith shop. In all, the British burn 333 buildings from Black Rock to 18-Mile-Creek in Hamburg before retreating back to Canada. But they leave a garrison at Fort Niagara.

Fort Niagara welcomes visitors year round. There have been forts at the site since the French explorer LaSalle established the first one in 1679.

The current fort dates to 1726 when the French built the ironically named "House of Peace," a stout stone building intended as a fortification, which remains one of the chief buildings at the present fort.

The name arose from the successful effort of the French to allay the suspicions of the fierce Iroquois, who were the most powerful outfit in the area at the time. The building today is known as "The French Castle."

The fort was greatly enlarged by the French during the French and Indian War. That didn't prevent it from being seized by the British under the command of Sir William Johnston in 1759.

The fort remained in British hands during the American revolution. From it, the infamous Butler's Rangers and its Iroquois allies staged raids on American farms and villages in New York and Pennsylvania.

It wasn't until 1786 that the fort was handed over to the Americans under treaty with Britain.

After its capture in the War of 1812, the British held it until it was returned to American hands in 1815, a few months following the end of the war.

During World War I, it served as an Army training camp. The original stone fort built by the French was lived in as late as 1925.

During World War II the fort was used to hold German prisoners of war. Although long obsolete as a military fortification, the U.S. Army continued to use it for various purposes until 1963 when the last soldiers moved out and the sructures and surrounding land was deeded to New York State.

Today, it is operated and maintained by the Old Fort Niagara Association.

It is opened year round. In the warm months, musket firing and other demonstrations of military life during the early period of the fort are given by guides dressed in the military uniform of the 1812 period.

To get there from Canada, follow the Niagara Parkway and cross the Lewiston-Queenston Bridge into the U.S. From there, take the Robert Moses Parkway north. It leads directly to the fort.

The Parkway can also be entered from Niagara Falls, N.Y.

An alternate route to the fort is Route 18 F from Lewiston, which borders the Niagara River. Just south of Youngstown, a plaque off Rt. 18F marks where the British and Canadians landed on the way to capture the stronghold.

Buffalo today shows little resemblance to the village burned during the War of 1812. There is little to remind visitors of its destruction during the war. Indeed, many residents are blissfully unaware of it.

But there is a plaque marking the location of the St. John house at 460 Main Street. The former location of the Lovejoy house across the street at 465 has a marker on the side of the building that tells visitors merely that it was there that the only civilian was killed during the torching of the city.

Visitors to Toronto will find several monuments and markers describing the events of the war which took place there including the taking of York --- twice -- by Americans. A plaque inside the entrance to the main Ontario Parliament building honors Gen. Drummond, who was in command during the burning of Buffalo.

Fort York, dating from before the War of 1812, is also in Toronto. The city, which is also an entertainment center rivaling New York City, is worth a visit of several days.

A description of the many monuments in Toronto and the city itself can be found in the many books about the city.

It is more than an hour drive from Niagara Falls -- unless traffic is unusually light and the driver has a very heavy foot.

As such it does not meet the requirement of this book that a drive to a battle site be less than an hour's drive, but it is a modern and dynamic city worth a visit, if you have the time.

Chapter Five

The Men In Gray -
Fort Erie, Chippawa and Lundy's Lane

By 1814, President Madison and most of his cabinet realize if the United States is to avoid further embarrassment on the battlefield, it will need younger, bolder military officers like Winfield Scott to lead American fighting forces.

So it is that March sees Scott, now at 28 the youngest brigadier general in the American army, once more in Buffalo.

The lost battle of Queenston and the discipline of the British troops steadfastly advancing in order in the face of cannon and musket fire has underscored in Scott's mind the need for training and disciplining the men under his command.

Spring comes late in western New York. It is usually wet and chilly,but Scott insists on military drills, ten hours a day, rain or shine. The recruits under him are taught to march in column and on line, to wheel and deploy, and to quickly load and reload their arms.

When summer comes, they are prepared — except for uniforms. The regulation blue uniforms have not arrived.

Instead, the men wear undyed gray.

The rough, gray uniforms are worn by most of Scott's men on July 3, 1814 as they make a night crossing of the Niagara and attack the garrison of Fort Erie. Among those leading the attack is the fire-eating Buffalo congressman and merchant, Peter Porter, who heads a contingent of more than a thousand militia and Iroquois. For the help of the Indians, Porter can thank the Seneca chief, Red Jacket, who has urged his followers to take part in the war on the side of the Americans.

The overall commander of the operation is Major General Jacob Brown. Like Scott, who is a friend, Brown is eager for battle. He is, moreover, comparatively young at 39 for a top commander.

Before sunset, the outnumbered British contingent at Fort Erie surrenders and Scott is ready to celebrate the Fourth by leading his troops down river to Chippawa where the British and Canadians await. British Gen. Riall, he who burnt Buffalo, heads the waiting troops.

The small Chippawa River must be crossed if the Americans are to continue northward toward Fort George.

There are no other bridges within miles. No army can seize the Niagara Peninsula without crossing the bridge.

Riall has his troops dig in on the north side of the river. On the south side, he places an artillery battery among the cluster of houses which make up the village of Chippawa.

As the Fourth ends, the test under fire of the new American troops is about to begin.

Riall decides to attack first. A flanking movement through the forest runs into a force of Pennsylvania militia and Indians led by Porter. The Americans in the forest flee.

Scott's troops are roughly equal in size to the 1,500 man British/Canadian force in front of them. They advance toward the bridge. Riall, noticing the gray uniforms, believes he is facing only a body of Buffalo militia who he expects will flee under fire.

But the men have learned well under Scott. Their morale and discipline are high. They continue their advance under fire from British cannon, halting only to reload their muskets and shoot.

"Those are regulars, by God," Riall shouts in surprise.

Cannon balls and grape shot tear into the advancing line, but the Americans close ranks and continue to march forward in perfect order.

American guns silence most of the British cannon. A cannon ball strikes the British magazine, blowing it up.

As the two forces draw within the length of two football fields from each other, Riall orders his men to charge.

They do. The charge is beaten back.

Now Scott orders a bayonet charge. The British break before the American troops and Riall orders a retreat.

The British soldiers flee across the bridge. The last ones rip up the planking to prevent the Americans from following.

In the past, American victories have come only when they outnumbered the British. Now, for the first time, the Americans have met a British force of equal size and forced them to withdraw. The British suffer 500 casualties, the Americans 325.

The victory is celebrated widely across the states. In recognition of the battle, in years to come to the present day, the uniform of U.S. cadets at West Point will be the gray worn by the Americans at Chippawa.

The American forces continue northward, past Niagara Falls to Queenston Heights which they retake without resistance. The plan is to attack Fort George from land and by water, reenforcing the land troops with men and supplies carried by the U.S. fleet anchored at Sackets Harbor on the far eastern end of Lake Ontario. After retaking Fort George, Brown believes he can occupy the entire Niagara Peninsula and retake the Upper Canada capitol of York.

But Commodore Isaac Chauncey has spent the war, not in fighting the British fleet on Lake Ontario, but by building more and larger ships. Fortunately for the Americans, the British naval officer, Sir James Yeo, who is in command of his nation's Great Lakes fleet, has a similar ship building mania.

Neither Yeo or Chauncey wants to risk losing their ships in battle.

Now Chauncey, pleading illness and fear of a British attack, refuses to take his ships westward. The planned bombardment of Fort George by naval guns will not take place. The expected reinforcements and supplies will not arrive.

As the American forces wait for the expected arrival of ships which will not come, they are subject to continued attacks by Canadians hostile to the invaders. In reprisal, the troops of Col. Isaac Stone, burn the Village of St. David, to the south of Fort George.

Gen. Brown, furious at the action, dismisses Stone, but the harm inflicted by the Americans strengthens the unity of Canadians against the invasion.

Without the siege guns, still on the boats in Sackets Harbor, the Americans cannot take the fort. The odds have also changed. Reinforcements have swelled the number of British troops to nearly four thousand. The number of Americans has diminished to about 2,600.

Brown moves his men back to Chippawa. From there, he hopes to resupply and reinforce his troops and move eastward to Burlington Heights. But there are British troops in the way and at Lundy's Lane and Portage Road in the present Niagara Falls another bloody battle awaits.

For it is there that Riall has placed nearly 4,000 troops and cannon on a knoll near a cemetery to block the Americans if they try to move west.

American scouts detect a British force on the knoll, but don't know their number. Scott, eager for a battle as usual, on a hot July 25 is heading toward Queenston with his 1,200 men who had been victorious at Chippawa. He is told by the congenial American-born hostess at a tavern near Table Rock at the Falls that the British have 800 regular troops plus 300 Canadian militia and Indians and only two cannons at Lundy's Lane. He marches west down Lundy's Lane and attacks, without waiting for reinforcements. But Scott has been misinformed. The Americans are outnumbered three to one, with seven cannons massed behind the center of the crescent-shaped British line. He does not know it, but Lt. General Gordon Drummond's veteran troops have arrived from York as reinforcements and are now beginning to form up.

On Scott's right is a deep woods where the present Canadian city of Niagara Falls now sprawls. He orders Major Thomas Jessup to slither through the woods with a battalion of men, flank the British from the right side and capture the enemy cannons. Scott will lead a frontal attack.

Jessup makes the flanking movement. He drives back two Canadian militia companies and two troops of dragoons. He captures Riall, badly wounded in the arm, which the general will lose. But Jessup is prevented from capturing the British cannons by enemy reinforcements who arrive on the battlefield from Queenston.

Scott's men are badly chewed up by musket fire and cannon fire. His attack fails. Darkness falls. Brown sends a brigade from Chippawa to reinforce Scott, but not the entire army.

He does not believe that the entire British army and most of the Canadian troops in the area are massed at Lundy's Lane.

The key to victory lies in the capture of the British cannon on the top of the hill. Brown, now at the battle scene, orders Col. James Miller to storm the hill with his 300 men. Under cover of darkness, they creep up the hill catching the British gunners by surprise as they fire into them. They capture the guns in a charge which wins the admiration of some British veterans of the wars against Napoleon, who admit they had never seen such determined charges. "The Americans charged to the very muzzles of the cannons," said one. "They actually bayoneted the gunners."

The British order a series of charges to retake the guns.They are repulsed after hard hand to hand fighting.

For two hours the opposing forces fight over the guns in darkness lit by musket fire, each being reinforced until there are no troops in reserve. The Royal Scots and the Glengarrys pour heavy fire on each other, both mistaking the other for the enemy. Americans fire on Americans.

Scott leads two failed charges into the British line, both times having horses shot under him. Morning dawns and the fighting continues. A spent cannon ball ploughs into Scott's right side, but he continues fighting until he is seriously wounded by a musket ball in his left shoulder.

Brown too is hurt by a spent cannon ball and a musket ball which pierces his right thigh. He turns the command over to Brigadier General Eleazar Ripley.

On the British side, Drummond is wounded in the neck. By noon, the firing has ended and the battlefield is filled only with the cries and moans of the wounded and hundreds of blood soaked dead. The Americans suffer 850 dead or wounded. Total British loses are about 875.

The Americans still hold the cannons, but with most of the horses dead, there is no way to move them. The British take back the guns.

Exhausted, the Americans withdraw from the field. The British are too battered and tired to follow after them.

The terrible battle, the bloodiest of the war so far, is a draw, although both sides claim victory.

The Americans retreat back to Fort Erie which becomes a 15-acre fortified camp anchored by the fort itself.

Drummond tries to force the Americans to abandon the fort and return to New York by sending 600 of his troops across the Niagara to destroy the American supplies at Black Rock and Buffalo. The Americans are waiting for the British behind a log barrier and their fire sends the enemy back across the river. If Fort Erie is to be taken, it must be taken by siege.

The bombardment of the fort begins on August 7. After a week, Drummond decides the fort has been weakened enough for his 3,000 men to breach the fort. He believes the Americans have 1,500 troops. He is wrong. They have double that number.

The attack begins at 2 a.m. on a rainy night. A thousand men are thrown into an attack on an American battery a half mile south of the fort located on a mound of sand 30 feet high dubbed Snake Hill. They are met with heavy fire from the Americans. They cannot shoot back because Drummond, hoping the attack will be a surprise, has ordered the men to remove the flints from their muskets to prevent a shot being fired accidentally. The British are to rely on their bayonets.

But not only do they not achieve surprise, the scaling ladders they carry are too short. They cannot get in within a musket's length of the Americans. Nevertheless, Lt. Col. Victor Fischer leads five charges up the wooden parapet erected to protect the gun crews. The 100 men who manage to penetrate the American defense are killed or captured. Others try to make an end run around the battery by wading in shallow water on the Lake Erie side of the fort and coming behind the cannons. But the Americans have prepared for that and the British led troops meet heavy fire. Many of the wounded are swept into the Niagara River by the fast currents. There many of them drown.

Fischer at last recalls his badly mauled troops. The attack on Snake Hill has failed. Outside the fort itself by the shore of the lake is another American cannon battery commanded by Lt. David Bates Douglass. The attack on it by 700 British troops was supposed to occur at the same time as the attack on Snake Hill, but they have been delayed and the attack doesn't come until nearly an hour later. When it does come, the Americans are prepared. A wall of fire lights up the attacking force as the cannons spout shot and muskets balls at point blank range on the charging red coats.

Again and again the British troops charge. Each time they are repulsed with heavy losses.

The attack on the fort, led by General Drummond's nephew, Lt. Col. William Drummond, is more successful. Twice the British force tries to scale the fort's walls with ladders. Each time it is driven back. But as smoke from Douglass's cannons obscures the vision of the defenders, the British succeed in scaling the north wall without being seen. Hand to hand fighting follows within the fort. The British are able to take possession of one side of the fort, but suddenly beneath their feet a powder magazine blows up. Flame shoots more than 100 feet in the air and with the shooting flame are stones, pieces of timber and parts of British bodies. In all, some 600 English troops are killed by the blast, the largest number of men killed in a single battle on Canadian soil. In all, the British force has suffered more than 900 killed or wounded — one-third of Gen. Drummond's army. The number of American killed and wounded is 130.

The survivors of the explosion flee the fort and seek safety behind their own lines. The attack on Fort Erie has failed.

The British wait for an American attack to smash their shattered army and drive the remnants away. It does not come.

Gaines is no Scott. He does not realize how weakened the British are. His men stay behind their fortifications.

Drummond's troops stay where they are. The siege continues. The British cannonade increases in fury.

It is, for Americans an historic month, this August. Nearly 500 miles east General Winder, surprised by the British in the embarrassing loss at Stoney Creek, is in charge of the defense of Washington, D.C. He is equally bumbling and surprised when the British attack and burn the nation's capitol and the White House. The British say it is in reprisal for the burnings of York, Newark and lesser Canadian communities on the Niagara Frontier.

But outside Baltimore, Fort McHenry, the key to that city's defense, holds out, despite a fierce and deadly British bombardment. A young poet, Francis Scott Key, watches the bombs bursting in air, and writes a poem commemorating the battle. It is set to the tune of an English drinking song. It is still sung this day. You undoubtedly have heard it. The anthem starts with the words, "Oh say can you see, by the dawn's early light, what so proudly we hailed in the twilight's last gleaming...."

Back in the Niagara Frontier, it is September and the British siege of Fort Erie continues. In an attempt to break it, on Sept. 17 an American force attacks two British batteries.

After hard and bloody fighting the attack fails. It creates 565 causalities on the British side, 511 on the American. The war on the Niagara frontier has once again reached a stalemate.

On Sept. 31 Drummond breaks off the siege and retreats back to Chippawa. A week later the Americans abandon the fort and return to the U.S. side of the river.

On Oct. 10 another American army of four thousand crosses the Niagara and advances to Chippawa where it skirmishes with the British. The plan is a repeat of the summer plan which again depends on Commodore Chauncey's arriving at the mouth of the Niagara with more men and supplies, combined with a bombardment of Fort George with naval cannon.

But once again, Chauncey refuses to endanger his ships. Drummond too awaits supplies and needed reinforcements from the British fleet commanded by Yeo, since fall rains and mud have made the roads nearly impassable. But Yeo too fails the army that needs him. Fearful of overloading his new grand ships, he carries only a few men and supplies. Both naval commanders think so highly of their ships that they fear loss or damage in battle. The war will end with two large war fleets on Lake Ontario rarely used because of the timidity of their commanders.

The fight has gone out of the two armies facing each other at Chippawa. Impeded by continual rain and his men cold and sick, Gen. George Izard, commanding the American army, decides to take his army back to New York State as the weather gets worse. Fort Erie is abandoned and blown up. By November, all American troops are back on American soil. Much blood has been spilled, thousands of lives have been lost, even more soldiers on both sides have lost limbs or other body parts or are prisoners, but nothing has been won, nothing decided.

THE best way to see what remains or marks the 1814 summer battles along the Niagara River is to drive the slow, but scenic Niagara Parkway (top posted speed – 40 mph) south (downstream) along the rapidly flowing stream. (It really isn't technically a river, but a natural channel in which Lake Erie flows into Lake Ontario.) Fort Erie is at the end of the 30 kilometer (about 20 miles) drive from Niagara Falls, Canada.

Taking the Queen Elizabeth Way from Niagara Falls is faster, but not as scenic. But if you do drive the QEW, get off at the Center Road exit (the last exit before the Peace Bridge) and turn right. Follow the signs to the fort.

From the U.S., cross the Peace Bridge, go off at the first exit and turn right at the next exit. Another right turn will take you to the Parkway. The rebuilt fort is less than half a mile away.

There is a modest admission charge to enter the fort. (As of this writing the charge was $7.50 for adults, $4.50 for children in Canadian dollars.) Once inside, in the summer costumed guides describe the fighting which took place as they lead guests through the buildings and show where the powder magazine blew up, taking so many British and Canadian lives. There is also musket and cannon firing, and preparing of food which would have been served in the early 19th century. Around Halloween, a night ghost tour is featured.

Drummond's efforts to capture the fort and its defense are enacted annually on the second weekend of August. The enactment includes a spectacular night battle. There are also recreations of the battles of Chippawa and Lundy's Lane on or near the anniversaries of those bloody encounters.

Most of the Lundy Lane battlefield is now obliterated by homes, streets and businesses. Near the top of the hill, which held the British cannon over which much of the battle was fought, is a city public grade school, Battlefield School. The few monuments and objects marking the site are in Drummond Hill Cemetery at the crest of the hill, which is at the intersection of Drummond Road and Lundy Lane. The most visible structure is the small Drummond Hill Presbyterian Church next to the cemetery.

Most of the gravestones in the cemetery mark the passings of those who lived long after the War of 1812. Near Lundy's Lane are raised grave markers identifying the remains of Unknown soldiers from both sides, a stone obelisk about 20 feet high, the grave and bust of Laura Secord, a small, brass statue of British Gen. Drummond on horseback and a couple of cannons from the period and several stacked cannonballs.

The cemetery itself must be entered from Buchner Road just off Drummond Road.

Chapter Six

Britain Abandons its Promise and Aims

The abandonment and destruction of Fort Erie by the Americans ended the fighting on the Niagara Frontier. The battles moved further east and south. On Lake Champlain, between New York and Vermont, an American fleet with a newly built vessel, the Saratoga, as its flagship, that September defeats a British fleet which has larger ships and greater firepower.

The naval victory endangers the supply line of a British invading army numbering 10,000 men which had crossed into upstate New York the previous week. The British rapidly withdraw, leaving many of their supplies behind.

Meanwhile, negotiations to end the war has been going on since early August between the Americans and British in Ghent, Belgium.

The first British demands are harsh and intolerable to the Americans. To get the needed help of their Indian allies during the war, the Brits have promised the Indians their own land taken from American territory. Now as requirement to end the war, the British demand that the Indian land be comprised of most of Ohio and the future states of Indiana, Michigan, Illinois and Wisconsin, a huge territory which has some 100,000 white setters already making their homes there.

That's not all, the British demand control of the Great Lakes and the right to freely sail on the Mississippi. On top of all that, they want to add a part of Maine to Canada.

Unsurprisingly, the American negotiators, who include John Quincy Adams and the leading U.S. war hawk, Henry Clay, refuse the British demands without hesitation. Under different conditions efforts to make peace might have ended. But the war has been financially costly to both sides. Both sides wish the conflict to end. Peace talks continue.

Britain abandons its promise to its Indian allies. There will be no new homeland for them, not in America and not in Canada. As weeks go by and talks continue, Britain, anxious to put this costly, senseless war behind it, withdraws all demands.

On Christmas eve, a peace treaty is signed by the negotiators.

Nothing has been won by either side. The treaty returns boundaries and conditions to what they were before the war.

Impressment of American seamen is no longer an issue.

Napoleon has been defeated and exiled to Elba. He will, of course, return to face his Waterloo, but England's pressing need for sailors has ended. And America no longer believes that Canadians secretly wish to be absorbed by their growing neighbor to the south.

Thousands of lives and limbs have been lost, cities and villages destroyed, families shattered, homes looted, grain fields ravaged, but there is little gain to justify the losses on either side.

Historians and other writers about the war will claim the conflict settled the matter of American independence for all time and showed the European powers that the United States was growing as a world power and its voice was to be heard.

"During the War of 1812, the United States would cast aside its cloak of colonial adolescence and...stumble forth onto the world stage. After the War of 1812, there was no longer any doubt that the United States of America was a national force to be reckoned with," claims Walter R. Borneman in his very readable and detailed book, *1812 the War that Forged a Nation.*

For Canadians, the war instilled a feeling of nationhood that was lacking among the newly arrived settlers. Never again will an American army invade its land. The Undefended Border will become a reality. Fort Niagara is returned to the U.S. Old Ironsides becomes a floating national symbol of American resistance to foreign domination and the nation has a national anthem -- although the music copies a British drinking song. The United States also has two new striking battle cries which will be repeated until the present time.

They are, of course, Perry's "We have met the enemy and they are ours," proclaimed after the Lake Erie victory; and Captain James Lawrence's dying plea: "Don't give up the ship!"

But, despite the peace treaty, there is another bloody chapter to be written in New Orleans. News of peace has not yet reached the American and British forces in the New World on Jan. 8, 1815, when a British army of nearly 8,000 launches a frontal attack on an entrenched but motley force of regular army troops, pirates and freed blacks under the command of Andrew Jackson. Most of the attacking force never reach American lines. They are slaughtered by cannon fire and bulletsfrom American rifles and muskets before they reach the U.S. lines or else save themselves by fleeing. The British lose more than 2,000 men; the Americans 70.

It is a great victory. It propels Jackson into the presidency. But the war has been over for a fortnight. It is a meaningless end to a pointless war.

The valor, courage and pain of the men and women on both sides who took part in the events which happened in the Niagara Frontier two hundred years ago has been largely passed over. But they were very real.

Further Reading

The most engrossing and comprehensive account of the War of 1812 is in the two volume work of a Canadian writer, the late Pierre Berton. Berton is a masterful story teller who ranks with Bruce Catton and Steven Ambrose in writing engaging prose using the accounts of those who were at the battles as sources.

Another two books are: *The Invasion of Canada,* that describes the events of 18121-13; and *Flames Across the Border*, that covers the years 1813-14. *1812* .

The War That Forged a Nation by Walter R. Borneman, is a well researched and very readable account.

A 96-page glossy book with full color pictures, photographs and illustrations is *The Invasion of Canada - Battles of the War of 1812* by Ronald J. Dale. (James Lorimer & Co., Toronto).

One of the many good books used for reference in writing this work is *The War of 1812 --A Forgotten Conflict* by Donald R. Hickey. (University of Illinois Press)

Other modern good books on the war: *The War of 1812: A Compact History,* Jacobs and Tucker.

War of 1812, John K. Mahon.

The War of 1812, Reginald Horsman.

The War of 1812, Harry L. Coles.

A graphic, illustrated account of the Battle of Lundy's Lane is: *Where Right and Glory Lead!* by another Canadian, Donald E. Graves.

David Nevin's well researched and griping novel, "1812," offers convincing and terrifying descriptions of the major battles of the war.

Some other books:

Prologue to War: England and the United States, 1805-1812, University of California Press, Bradford Perkins.

History of the United States of America during the Administations of Jefeson and Madison, Henry Adams.

The Pictorial Field-Book of the War of 1812, Benson J. Lossing.

Amongst My Best Men: African Americans and the War of 1812. The Perry Group, 1996. Gerald T. Altoff.

The Iroquois in the War of 1812. Carl Benn.

*The War of 1812.*University of Chicago Press. Henry I. Coles.

The Invasion of Canada: The Battles of the War of 1812, Ronald Dale.

Agent of Destiny: The Life and Times of General Winfield Scott. Free Press., 1977. John S.D. Eisenhower.

Red Coats and Grey Jackets: The Battle of Chippawa, 1814. Dundurn Press, Toronto, 1994. Donald E. Graves.

Portraits & Photographs

Gen Brock was killed trying to retake cannon after it was lost to U.S. forces. It was here that Winfred Scott and other remaining Americans were taken prisoner by the British/Canadian forces after reinforcements refused to cross the Niagara. The Brock monument is nearby.

Bust of Laura Secord marks where the heroine of the Ware of 1812 is buried. The spot is not in Queenston, Ontario, but in the cemetery marking where the Battle of Lundy's lane was fought.

Monument to the men killed during the bloody battle of Lundy's Lane.

U.S. and Canadian Boy and Girl Scouts take part in a reenactment of the capture of Fort George by American forces.

Lightning Source UK Ltd.
Milton Keynes UK
19 December 2010

164603UK00005B/16/P